Caddo

by Heather Kissock

LG (K-3)
ATOS 4.0
0.5 pts
Non-Fiction

139824 EN

American Indian
Art and Culture

CADDO

Heather Kissock
and Rachel Small

WEIGL PUBLISHERS INC.
"Creating Inspired Learning"
www.weigl.com

Published by Weigl Publishers Inc.
350 5th Avenue, 59th Floor
New York, NY 10118

Website: www.weigl.com
Copyright ©2011 Weigl Publishers Inc.

Library of Congress Cataloging-in-Publication Data

Kissock, Heather.
 Caddo : American Indian art and culture / Heather Kissock and Rachel Small.
    p. cm.
 Includes index.
 ISBN 978-1-60596-979-4 (hardcover : alk. paper) -- ISBN 978-1-60596-980-0 (softcover : alk. paper) -- ISBN 978-1-60596-981-7 (e-book)
 1. Caddo art--Juvenile literature. 2. Caddo Indians--Material culture--Juvenile literature. 3. Caddo Indians--Social life and customs--Juvenile literature. I. Small, Rachel. II. Title.
 E99.C12K57 2011
 305.897'93--dc22

                    2010005334

Printed in the United States of America in North Mankato, Minnesota
1 2 3 4 5 6 7 8 9 0 14 13 12 11 10

042010
WEP264000

Photograph and Text Credits
Cover: Courtesy, National Museum of the American Indian, Smithsonian Institution (26/5161); Alamy: pages 5, 13, 22L; Bata Shoe Museum: page 9B (P93.100); Corbis: pages 6, 7, 8, 17; Dreamstime: pages 4, 10L, 11R, 22R, 23; Getty Images: pages 10M, 10R, 11L, 11M, 15, 23; Courtesy, National Museum of the American Indian, Smithsonian Institution: pages 9T (2/2684), 9M (23/2026) and (2/2690), 14B (2/2189); Nativestock: pages 12, 20, 21; Oklahoma State Historical Society: page 14T (19344.46.19), 16 (627).

Every reasonable effort has been made to trace ownership and to obtain permission to reprint copyright material. The publishers would be pleased to have any errors or omissions brought to their attention so that they may be corrected in subsequent printings.

All of the Internet URLs given in the book were valid at the time of publication. However, due to the dynamic nature of the Internet, some addresses may have changed, or sites may have ceased to exist since publication. While the author and publisher regret any inconvenience this may cause readers, no responsibility for any such changes can be accepted by either the author or the publisher.

PROJECT COORDINATOR Heather Kissock

DESIGN Terry Paulhus

ILLUSTRATOR Martha Jablonski-Jones

Contents

The People

The Caddo Indians **traditionally** lived on the southern plains of the United States. In the past, Caddo lands were spread along the rivers and lakes of Louisiana, Arkansas, Oklahoma, and east Texas.

When Europeans arrived in these areas, the Caddo moved to what is now the western part of Texas. Over time, they moved to Oklahoma, where most Caddo still live today. There are about 4,000 Caddo living in Oklahoma.

NET LINK

Find out how the word "Texas" relates to the Caddo at **www.texasindians.com/caddo.htm**.

Caddo Homes

HOUSES

Traditionally, the Caddo lived in cone-shaped houses. Their homes were built with sticks and poles. The frame was then covered in **thatched** grass.

The Caddo built two homes for their families. The winter home had a roof and walls. The summer home had only a roof. This allowed the Caddo to stay cool in the hot summer months.

TEMPLE MOUNDS

The Caddo built their villages around a special mound used for religious ceremonies. This was called the temple mound.

Caddo Clothing

SKIRTS AND TOPS

The women wore skirts and tops that looked like **ponchos**. These clothes were made from animal skins and woven plant **fibers**.

BREECHCLOTHS AND LEGGINGS

Caddo men wore breechcloths and leggings. Most clothing was made from animal skins, such as deer, bison, and bear. Sometimes, the Caddo would decorate the skins with beads.

HEADGEAR

Some Caddo men wore hair roaches on their head. These were long strips of porcupine hair that ran from the front to the back of the head. Women decorated their hair with ornaments, such as headbands.

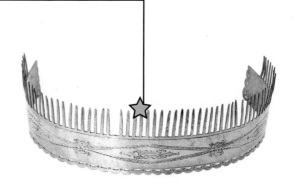

JEWELRY

Both men and women wore jewelry. Men wore earrings, necklaces, feathers, and nose rings. Women wore earrings, necklaces, bracelets, and rings. Many Caddo also had tattoos.

MOCCASINS

The Caddo wore moccasins on their feet. These were made from animal hides. They often were decorated with beads or porcupine quills.

Hunting and Gathering

DEER
The Caddo hunted deer and used the meat for food. Deer meat could be cooked on its own, put in stews, or dried for winter use.

NUTS
The area where the Caddo lived had many nut trees. They gathered nuts, such as pecans, to use in their cooking.

SALT
The Caddo gathered salt from springs and **seeps**. It was used to flavor foods and was traded for other items.

The Caddo were best known as farmers. They cleared patches of land in the woods where they lived to plant crops. They also relied on food plants found in nature, such as walnut and pecan trees. Men would hunt animals in the area.

CORN

Corn was the Caddo's most important crop. The Caddo grew many different kinds of corn. It was often pounded down to make cornbread.

PUMPKINS

Pumpkins were a common crop for the Caddo. As well as a food source, pumpkins would be dried and cut into strips to make mats.

BEANS

The Caddo relied on beans for food. They would dry beans so that they could be stored and eaten during the winter.

Caddo Tools

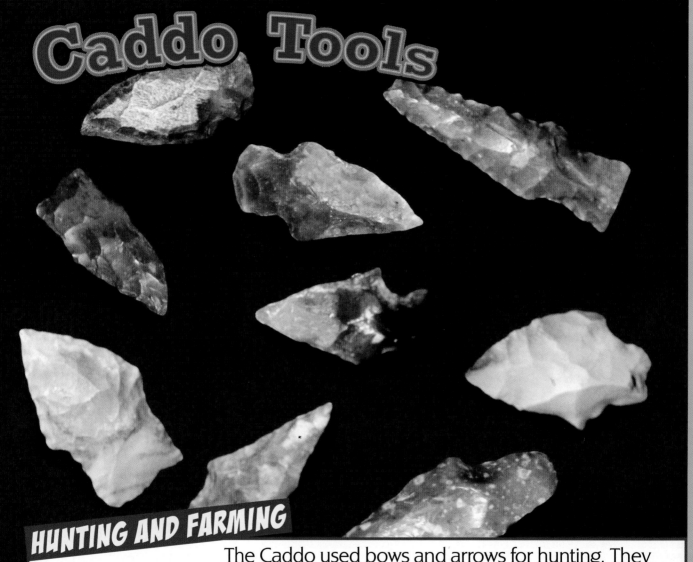

HUNTING AND FARMING

The Caddo used bows and arrows for hunting. They used shovels and other tools to farm the land. These tools were made from materials found in nature, such as wood, animal bones, shells, and stone.

FISHING

Baskets were a useful tool for fishing. Basket traps were placed in the water. When fish swam into a trap, a door shut them inside.

NET LINK

See how basket traps are made at **www.museum.state.il.us/RiverWeb/harvesting/ harvest/fish/tools_techniques/basket_traps.html**.

Moving from Place to Place

FOOT

In the past, the Caddo went barefoot when traveling on land. Later, they began making moccasins to help protect their feet.

Caddo Ideas

The Caddo also used rafts to travel on water. The rafts were made of wooden poles that were bound together.

CANOES

The Caddo used canoes to travel by water. They built canoes from hollow logs. To hollow a log, the wood inside the log was removed. These were known as dugout canoes.

Caddo Music and Dance

Music and dance were an important part of Caddo life. Caddo dances were performed to the beat of a drum. Drummers sat around one big drum that they played together. Sometimes, the drum was filled with water to create a special sound.

The Caddo had about 20 dances they performed. There were more than 200 songs to accompany the dances.

NET LINK

Watch the Caddo perform the turkey dance at **http://caddolegacy.com/Caddo SongsandDances.aspx**.

Why Arrows Have Feathers

One day, a baby hawk fell from its nest. A boy came along and felt sorry for the hawk. He picked it up and took it back to his village. There, he nursed the hawk back to health.

The hawk was grateful to the boy and decided to stay with him even when his health improved. The two became good friends and would do many things together.

One day, the boy was carving wood into arrows. When he shot the arrows, however, they did not fly straight. The boy never hit his target.

The hawk had an idea to make the arrows fly straight. He plucked some feathers and gave them to the boy. The boy attached the feathers to the end of the arrows and tried shooting. This time, the arrows flew straight and hit their mark.

The boy shared this tip with the rest of the village. Soon, the news spread to other villages, and they began to attach feathers to their arrows.

Caddo Art

The Caddo were well known for their woodwork and basket making. Masks were carved from wood and used during ceremonies. Baskets were made from river cane, as well as grasses and barks. They were used to store food.

The Caddo were especially skilled at pottery. They carved detailed designs in many of their pieces. The pottery was used for daily tasks, such as cooking food.

Make a Clay Pot

Materials
self-drying modeling clay, such as Plasticine
a popsicle stick

Steps
1. Work the clay in your hands until it is soft and flexible.
2. Mold the clay into a pot shape.
3. Using the popsicle stick, draw a pattern into your pot.
   Be careful not to squish the pot, or it will lose its shape.
4. Place your pot in a safe place to dry.
5. Once dry, the pot is complete. Use the pot to hold beads,
   buttons, pennies, or other objects.

Glossary

fibers: long, slender threads

ponchos: cloaks that have a hole in the center that a person's head can come through

seeps: places where liquid comes out from the ground to form a pool

thatched: a rooftop made from plants

traditionally: related to beliefs, practices, and objects that have been passed down from one generation to the next